The Drummer

One evening, a young drummer saw three pieces of white linen kept near a lake shore. 'What fine linen,' he thought and kept one of the pieces with him. Later at night when he was sleeping, he heard a voice saying, 'Drummer! Drummer! Wake up!' He woke up. 'Return my shift you had picked up from the lake shore,' said the voice. 'Who are you?' asked the drummer.

‘I am a mighty king’s daughter,’ said the voice. ‘But a witch has kept me captive up on the glass mountain. Without my shift, I cannot return.’ The drummer then held out the shift which was hastily snatched. ‘Can I help you to escape?’ asked the drummer. ‘Only if you can climb the glass mountain,’ said the voice. ‘Tell me the way,’ said the drummer. ‘The road goes through the forest where the giants live,’ said the voice.

Next morning, the drummer picked up his drum and without fear went into the forest beating his drum loudly. Soon, a giant came before him. 'Why are you beating your drum so loudly?' roared the giant. 'I am showing the way to the thousands who are following me. They want to kill you,' said the drummer calmly. 'I will trample them like ants,' roared the giant. 'Well, they all carry a hammer of steel and can easily kill you,' warned the drummer.

Hearing this, the giant became fearful. 'All right, I will leave you and your folks alone,' said the giant. 'Is there anything else I can do for you?' 'Carry me to the glass mountain. I shall then ask my followers to return,' said the drummer.
Immediately, the giant placed the drummer on his shoulder and started walking. The drummer, meanwhile, continued beating his drum. The giant thought that beating the drum was a signal to the people to return.

In no time, the giant reached the glass mountain. He placed the drummer near the foot of the mountain and returned to the forest. The mountain was huge and its sides were as smooth as glass. 'How will I climb it?' wondered the drummer. Just then, he heard two men arguing fiercely. The drummer asked them, 'Why are you arguing?' 'It is because of that saddle,' said one of the men pointing to a saddle.

The drummer learnt that the saddle was magical. It could take whoever sat on it anywhere by merely wishing. Both these men rode on it in turns but now they were fighting to decide whose turn it was.

'I will resolve the matter,' said the drummer. Then he walked a short distance and stuck a white rod in the ground. He returned to the men and said, 'Whosoever gets there first shall ride the saddle.'

But the moment the two men started running, the drummer swung himself on the saddle and wished to reach on top of the glass mountain. In a flash he was there. On top of the mountain stood an old stone house between a large pond and a forest. The drummer knocked on the door. An old witch opened the door.

'I want food and a bed to sleep in,' said the drummer.

'Only if you will perform three tasks for me,' said the witch. The drummer agreed.

The next morning, the witch gave the drummer a thimble and said, 'Empty out the pond with this thimble by nightfall. Also, sort all the fishes in the water according to their size and kind.' It was an impossible task! By noon, the drummer was tired. Then, a maiden came up to him and asked, 'What troubles you?' The drummer told her why he was there and also about the witch's task. 'I will help you,' said the maiden. 'You must rest.'

No sooner was the drummer asleep that the maiden turned her wishing ring and said, 'Rise water. Fish come out.' Immediately, the water evaporated. The fish sprang on the shore and laid themselves side by side according to their size and kind. When the drummer woke up, his task was completed. Then, the maiden said, 'One fish is lying alone. When the witch comes tonight and asks you why it is so, you must throw it on her face.' At night when the witch came, the drummer did likewise.

Next day, the witch said, 'Cut the forest, split the wood into logs, and pile them up before nightfall.' She then gave him an axe made of lead. But by noon, the drummer was unable to cut a single tree. Again, the maiden helped him. She turned her wishing ring. Immediately, the whole forest fell down, the wood split, and arranged itself in heaps. When the drummer woke up, she said, 'One bough remains alone. When the witch asks you about it, give her a blow with it.'

Later, the drummer did as he was told and the witch merely laughed. Next morning, she asked the drummer to arrange all the wood in one heap and set fire to it. But how could a single man bring an entire forest together! Yet again, the maiden came and helped him. While an enormous pile of logs burned, the maiden said, 'When the witch comes, do all she asks without fear. Then, seize her and throw her into the fire.

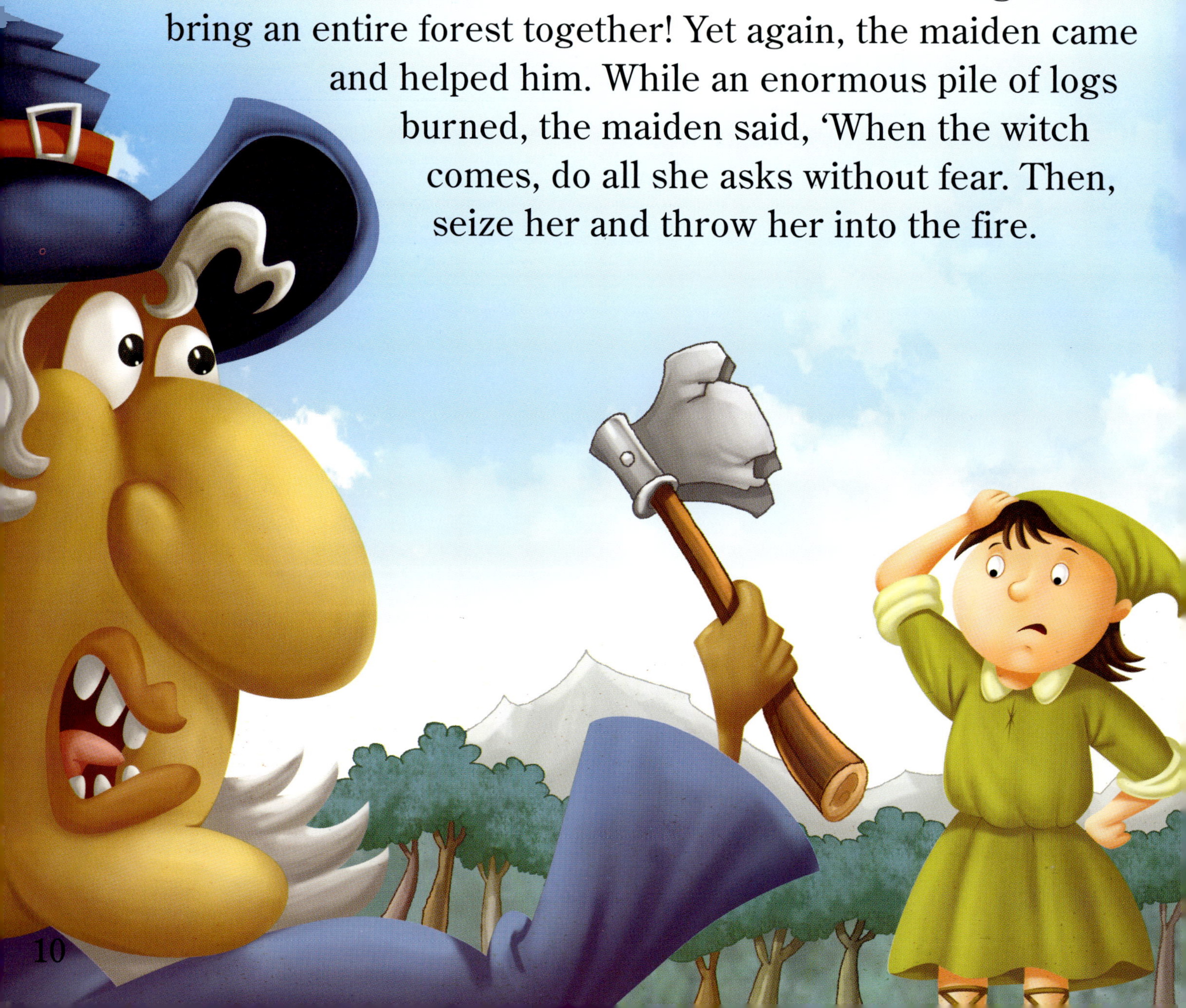

At night, the witch came and said, 'I see that one log is not burning. Jump in and set it on fire. Without hesitation, the drummer jumped amidst the flames. He did not burn at all! He took out the log and kept it on the ground. Immediately, it transformed into the beautiful maiden, who had helped him. She was the king's daughter. 'She isn't safe yet,' laughed the witch wickedly. But immediately, the drummer seized the witch and threw her amidst the flames. The witch died.

Then, the king's daughter thinking how the drummer had risked his life to save her, agreed to marry him. Then, after gathering precious jewels from the witch's house, the maiden turned her wishing ring and they were standing before the town gate. 'I want to meet my parents and give them the news of our marriage,' said the drummer. 'But be careful,' cautioned the king's daughter. 'Do not kiss your parents on the right cheek or you will forget everything.'

But in his joy, the drummer kissed his parents on the right cheek. At once, he forgot about the king's daughter. The drummer made a splendid castle. Soon, a wedding was arranged for the drummer. Meanwhile, the king's daughter who had been waiting for the drummer understood what must have happened. Her heart was filled with sorrow. One day, she learnt of the drummer's wedding. 'I will try to win back his heart,' said the king's daughter filled with determination.

On the first day of the wedding ceremonies, the king's daughter arrived wearing a dress that seemed to be made of sunbeams. The bride could not resist and asked her if she would sell her dress. 'Only if you will let me stay outside the groom's room,'

said the king's daughter. The bride agreed but she mixed a sleeping portion into the wine of the drummer. And while the king's daughter sang outside the groom's room about why he had forgotten her, the drummer slept on. Next day, she arrived wearing a dress made of moonbeams.

The king's daughter repeated her request to the bride in exchange of the dress. But again her efforts went in vain. However, the wedding guests had heard her lamentations and they told the drummer about them. On the third evening, when she once again sat outside the groom's room, he heard her and his memory returned. 'How could I have acted so unfaithfully!' cried the drummer. That day the drummer and the king's daughter got married. As for the drummer's first bride, she received the dresses as compensation.